PERFORMANCE FAVORITES

Volume 1

Band Arrangements Correlated with Essential Elements® Band Method Book 2

ISBN 978-1-4234-5781-7

HAL•LEONARD®
7777 W. BLUEMOUND RD. P.O. BOX 13819 MILWAUKEE, WI 53213

00860193

AFRICAN SKETCHES
(Based on African Folk Songs)

Bb TRUMPET 1

JAMES CURNOW (ASCAP)

BARRIER REEF
Overture For Band

Bb TRUMPET 1

JOHN HIGGINS (ASCAP)

D.C. al Fine
(with Repeat)

DO YOU HEAR WHAT I HEAR

Bb TRUMPET 1

Words and Music by
NOEL REGNEY and GLORIA SHAYNE
Arranged by MICHAEL SWEENEY

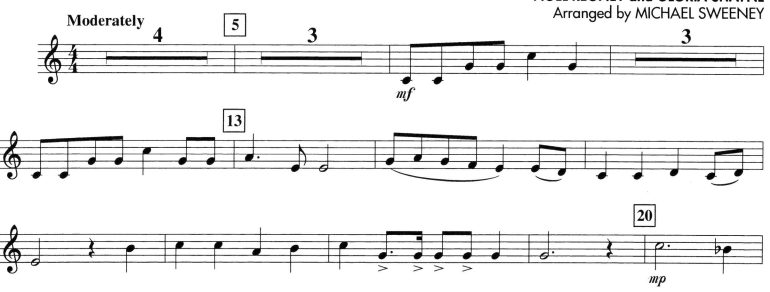

REGIMENTAL HONOR

B♭ TRUMPET 1

JOHN MOSS (ASCAP)

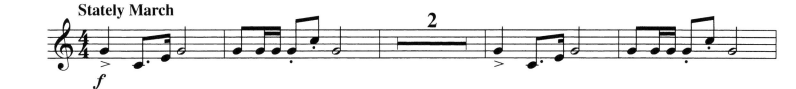

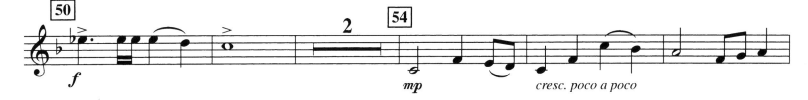

Recorded by **BLOOD, SWEAT, & TEARS**
SPINNING WHEEL

Words and Music by
DAVID CLAYTON THOMAS
Arranged by MICHAEL SWEENEY

Bb TRUMPET 1

Moderate Rock

00860193

THE STREETS OF MADRID

Bb TRUMPET 1

JOHN MOSS

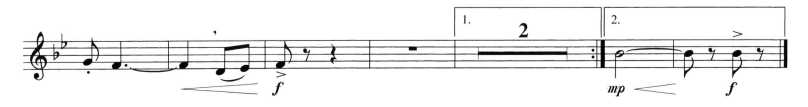

YOU'RE A GRAND OLD FLAG

B♭ TRUMPET 1

Words and Music by GEORGE M. COHAN
Arranged by PAUL LAVENDER

BRITISH MASTERS SUITE

B♭ TRUMPET 1

Arranged by JOHN MOSS

I. Marching Song

GUSTAV HOLST

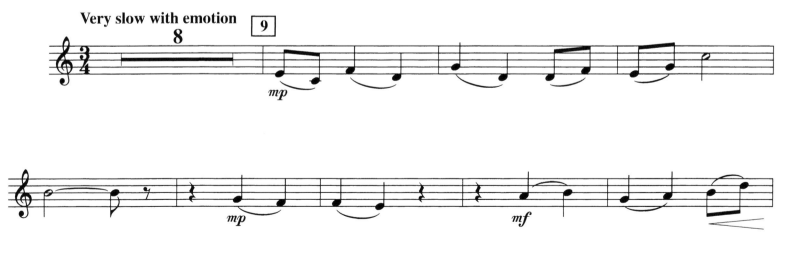

II. Nimrod (From "Enigma Variations")

EDWARD ELGAR

III. Sine Nomine

RALPH VAUGHAN WILLIAMS

ELVES' DANCE
(From The Nutcracker)

PETER I. TCHAIKOVSKY
Arranged by PAUL LAVENDER

Bb TRUMPET 1

00860193

FIREBIRD SUITE - Finale

Bb TRUMPET 1

IGOR STRAVINSKY
Arranged by JOHN MOSS

00860193

GAELIC DANCES

Bb TRUMPET 1

Arranged by JOHN MOSS

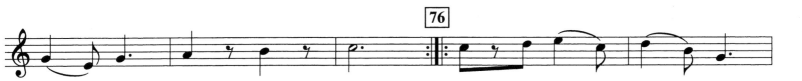

00860193

IRISH LEGENDS

Bb TRUMPET 1

JAMES CURNOW (ASCAP)

ON BROADWAY

Words and Music by BARRY MANN, CYNTHIA WEIL,
MIKE STOLLER and JERRY LEIBER
Arranged by MICHAEL SWEENEY

Bb TRUMPET 1

00860193

Written for the 100th Anniversary Celebration of the Modern Olympic Games

SUMMON THE HEROES
(For Tim Morrison)

Bb TRUMPET 1

By JOHN WILLIAMS
Arranged by MICHAEL SWEENEY

TWO CELTIC FOLKSONGS

(The Maids of Mourne Shore • The Star of the County Down)

Celtic Folksongs
Arranged by PAUL LAVENDER

Bb TRUMPET 1